Grieving sucks

Grieving Sucks
(Or Does it?)

By

Betty Freeman Haines

InterWorld Publishing Inc.

ISBN: 978-0-9834441-4-5

Cover : Design/Author portrait by Cindi Delaney (of Delaney Studios). Sunset photo by Walt Haines

Table of Contents

To my two Richards

Who were always there when I so desperately needed them

&

To my dearest friend BJ

Who truly meant it when she said, "I'm there for you 24/7".

She never wavered – even during 3am phone calls

Foreword

My husband and I loved watching sunrises and sunsets. When we were not traveling, it was our morning ritual that he rose early (usually before daybreak), brewed our morning coffee (a custom blend that he ordered from Amazon.com), poured it into our special mugs (huge ones that we purchased on our first trip to Zion National Park), and, flavored it perfectly to our taste (just as his buddy Terry Kelly had taught him to do). Then, he woke me; while I washed my face and put on my robe, he set out our chairs (facing east) in the front of the open garage door, turned on the radio and tuned it to KONY so that we could enjoy the *Carl and Marty In The Morning* show while we drank our coffee. By the time he had this done, I stumbled out the door, in search of a good morning kiss and caffeine.

We sat sipping coffee, talking with each other, laughing with Carl and Marty, waving to neighbors who drove or walked by and watching the sun rise over our beautiful southwest foothills and mesas.

Unless wind or heat made it impractical, our evenings were spent on our back patio. Here we sipped Southern Sweet Tea or Southern Comfort and watched the sun set behind Flat-top Mesa.

When my husband died, I stopped drinking coffee, avoided the garage (except to enter and exit the car), lost interest in "Carl and Marty", seldom saw my neighbors and paid no attention to sunrises or sunsets.

I was totally unprepared for the profound grief brought on by the loss of my husband; I learned very quickly that GRIEVING SUCKS. It took much longer for me to learn that profound grief can teach many valuable lessons. I'm beginning to accept that maybe, just maybe, the lessons I learned were worth much of the pain that I endured. I still say that GRIEVING SUCKS; however, I also ponder the question - OR DOES IT?

I doubt that I will ever again sit in my open garage, drink coffee and listen to Carl and Marty; that was, and will remain, part of the life I shared with my husband. However, I'm once again watching sunrises and sunsets, and savoring the sipping of

Sweet Tea or Southern Comfort. I take the time to treasure memories of the past, enjoy the present and plan for the future.

My brother-in-law, Walton P. Haines, an accomplished photographer, took the picture of the sunset that is featured on the front cover of this book. It is his way of immortalizing his brother's love of sunsets. Thanks WP, it is a most fitting tribute to your brother.

SECTION I

GRIEVING SUCKS

Introduction

At the time of my husband's sudden death I was no stranger to grief. Mistakenly, I believed that I was prepared for the grief that was to follow. I had experienced grief on a number of occasions; plus, I had researched the subject in conjunction with a curriculum design project .

My prior experiences with grief included:

- The death of my fraternal Grandma (Idell) who helped raise me. Her passing hurt deeply. I was a young newlywed at the time of her passing; I had a demanding job to keep me busy and a new husband to console me. My new husband even provided me with a new puppy to cuddle and care for when I was sad. Additionally, I took comfort in the fact that she was going to the reward that her strong Southern Baptist faith promised. I knew that she expected me to deal with the loss and get on with life; so, I did.

- The death of my Mama (Melba). This loss made me angry. I was furious with my Mama for dying; *how dare she leave me like this with no warning?* I knew that she suffered from congestive heart failure; but, in my heart, I felt confident that she would beat that specific problem. She had a long history of overcoming health problems; besides, she was too young to die. I was angry with God; how dare He let my Mama die. Ultimately, the anger passed and with its passing, I was again able to cherish the relationship my Mama and I had shared and to treasure memories of her.

- The death of my Daddy (RC). This caused immediate, physical pain – a sharp stabbing pain in the mid-section -   followed by an aching feeling of abandonment. Daddy's passing was not the surprise that my Mama's had been. It was, however, heart wrenching in a way that nothing else had ever been. With the loss of Daddy, I became an orphan; this left me feeling utterly alone, even in the middle of family. Daddy was my rock and my hero. Winning his approval or putting a look of pride in his eyes meant more to me than riches or fame.

- The death of my younger brother (Clay). I was rocked to the core when Clay died; he was much too young and involved in this life to leave it. He had beaten cancer once and seemed to be winning his second battle with the disease. I railed at God for taking him: *this isn't how it is supposed to be - he is younger than me – we have joint projects we are working on – we have so much more to share and so many more roads to travel together.* For months I was mired in sorrow and unable to let go of my grief. I begged daily for him to come back to us. Thanks to the love and understanding of my husband and my nephew, Gary, I was eventually able to release my brother to become God's Jazzman and get on with my life.

Losing my husband was entirely different than any of my previous losses. We were the couple who laughed at the absurdity of the phrase *too much togetherness.* We were soulmates and in love; we were the very best of friends. For us, too much togetherness didn't exist. Neither of us was dependent on the other for survival; we didn't need to be together to make life complete; we **wanted** to be together because we found life more exciting and enjoyable that way.

We maintained our home, raised our family, went back to college, traveled, and socialized together. For more than thirty years, we worked at the same company, often, for the same manager. Our work mates jokingly referred to us as *the Twofers* - as in *two for one.* When someone new joined the department, our co-workers informed them: "If you ask Betty for help, you're gonna get Vern's input whether you want it or not. If you ask Vern for help, well then, Betty is automatically part of the package".

To nobody's surprise, when we retired we became an even closer team. Oh, we had our spats; sometimes they escalated to heated arguments, but they were few, far between and short lived. Neither of us held a grudge; forgiving and forgetting was easy for us.

Many times we were warned that it wasn't wise for us to spend so much time together. Folks said, "One of you has to go first. If each of you has established independent interests and friendships, it will be easier for the one left behind."

Yes, one of us did go first. Sadly for me, my husband was the one. Yes, losing him was every bit as hard as folks had predicted. I suspect that the mechanics of managing my life as a widow, would have been easier if I had been more independent during my husband's life time. Nonetheless, I have no regrets. If we had chosen to spend less time together, a lot of wonderful memories wouldn't have been made. As for the grieving, nothing would have made any difference. **Absolutely nothing could have prepared me for this loss or made the grieving any easier.**

Grieving is a complex emotional experience; it is greatly influenced by the relationship between the one who has passed on and the one left behind. The manner in which one endures and/or muddles through the grieving process is different for each of us; however, one thing remains universal; **GRIEVING SUCKS.**

Chapter One

Grieving Sucks - it makes you numb.

"Mrs. Haines, your husband isn't going to make it. Do you want to come into the room and whisper your goodbyes?"

I hear the words, nod and, calm as a cucumber, I follow the doctor into the room. I think I'm holding up well; the reality is I'm numb; but, I don't yet know that.

Following a last hug and final whispered: "I love you, I'll be OK, you go in peace." The doctor leads me into the hall. I tell myself that everything is OK and I'm in control. Ha! I'm in control only because, deep down inside, I fully expect that at any minute my husband will appear and tell me what to do next. He has always watched out for me that way. He just just quietly steps in and makes things right.

After standing in the hall for a few minutes, it begins to sink in that my husband isn't coming to rescue me this time and my mind goes into overdrive as I struggle to grasp and deal with the situation:

OMG! Do I embrace the doctor who is expressing his condolences? Why is the hospital director standing here in front of me? Is this normal hospital procedure? Perhaps, it is because she is a friend to my husband & me? Do I hug her? Am I allowed to cry? Am I expected to cry? Why are all those people behind her staring at me? **What in the hell am I supposed to do?**

Before my mind can even fully formulate the above questions, my thoughts are interrupted by someone asking me an even more startling question. *"Mrs. Haines, what do you want us to do with the body?"*

Note to readers: You better know the answer to this question; long before you even figure out why you are standing in the middle of a hallway staring at a hospital director and emergency room staff, somebody is gonna demand the answer and "I don't know" just doesn't work; they keep telling you they have to have an answer. They are nice, they are *"sorry for your loss"* but they have to have an answer.

Some kind person took pity on me and made the decision to call to a local morgue. In this case, not the right decision; but, at least it was a decision and I am grateful to whoever made it for me.

The hospital director led me into a conference room so that I didn't have to stand in the hallway making my calls. Calls? Whom do I call? What do I say? Do I have to call every family member? Even the ones I don't like? Can't I just call my buddy BJ and see if she can make this all go away? BJ will tell them that my husband isn't dead and they just need go back in there and fix it so that I can take him home.

My first call is totally illogical. Instinctively, I reach out to an old friend of mine; one that my husband doesn't know well. I figure that telling this person of his demise won't cause as much pain as talking to family members. Finally, I gather the courage to talk with my husband's brother, my oldest son and my lifelong friend BJ; thankfully, they take on the chore of notifying others for me.

A hospital employee, who is a stranger to me, is kind enough to see to it that I'm driven home and that someone follows in my car. That kind soul brews me a cup of tea, settles me into a comfortable chair and lets herself out of my home. For the next 10 hours I just sat there. I didn't eat, drink, turn on the TV or go to the bathroom; I just sat mindlessly numb, waiting for someone to tell me what to do next. Finally, my oldest son arrived and I was able to get up and greet him.

Chapter Two

Grieving Sucks – you come unraveled

I'm at loose ends; in a matter of minutes, the world that Vern and I so lovingly created has come apart at the seams; it has unraveled and left me alone and exposed to the world with no shelter. -Journal entry

I was not prepared for how quickly or acutely I experienced the sensation that life was spiraling out of control. One minute I was a wife, happily living with my husband, in the snug little corner of the world that we called home; the next minute, I was a widow with a house full of guest needing attention. I had not yet grasped the idea that there was no *we*, so how could I be expected to remember where *we* kept the air bed, what *we* had in the freezer, or where *our* good china was stored. I didn't want to embarrass my husband by feeding folks on our "every day dishes." Finally it hit me there was no longer any *"we"* and my husband could no longer be embarrassed by any social blunder that I committed.

Without a doubt, this moment – the moment when I realized there was no longer any *"**WE**"* - was the most frightening and horrifying moment of my life. Did I cry, scream, or ask for a hug? No, I just stood in the middle of my kitchen, surrounded by loved ones, and silently became a lost and lonely soul who has no idea how I would survive.

Then, I remembered that my husband and I had made a pact that whichever spouse survived the longest would **_not_** fall apart and become a burden to our loved ones. So, I hitched up my big girl panties and got on with it! "Getting on with it" was no easy task and it is only by the grace of God, sheer will, and the strong desire to honor the last pact that my husband and I made that I was able to do so.

Chapter Three

Grieving Sucks - everybody has advice

Every damned body wants me to read a book, talk to a minister, or listen to the advice they offer. All I need is a hug. Why can't anyone see that I need a hug? –Journal entry

It started as I was making calls to notify folks of my husband's passing. The immediate response of one dear friend was, "Oh, I have just what you need, I'm going to send you a book about how to handle this." That was the first in a long chain of advice, suggestions, book recommendations, and gifts of books that seemed to come in even faster than covered dishes and sympathy cards. I understood that the suggestions were heart felt and well intended. Likewise, I knew that these people truly wanted to comfort me. Unfortunately, I was too distraught to fully comprehend the advice and the few things that I attempted to read offered no help. The books were long on the *process* advice and woefully short on or devoid of addressing *feelings* or providing *inspiration*.

It is day four of widowhood and nobody has yet offered to hold me while I cry. God, I wish I could tell somebody how much I hurt and how I hunger for a few moments shelter in caring arms - but, they are all wrapped up in their own hurt and I won't add to that. *Journal entry*

Chapter Four

Grieving Sucks – you have no back-up

There is no way that I can handle this. Vern is my rock, my back-up, and my protector. When I hurt, his immediate reaction is to "fix it". Well, this needs fixin'; he is not around and I haven't a clue how to fix that or anything else. – *Journal entry*

When lovers and soul mates are in a long term intimate relationship, a third unique entity inevitability develops. As the relationship moves from the lust phase to true intimacy, that third entity becomes as natural as breathing and as comfortable as an old shoe. This entity grows and evolves as each partner begins to do things to accommodate the style and comfort of the other. Most of the time there is no discussion of who does what and why; it is just something that couples do.

Example: I hate vacuuming the floor. I will put it off until dust bunnies begin multiplying in the corners of the room. Therefore, early in our relationship my husband took over the vacuuming. On the other hand, my husband pretended that the commode brush had never been invented; so, cleaning the bathroom became my job. Also, he appeared to fear the washing machine, and would literally wear his "cleanest pair of dirty socks" before he would go near the darned thing. I took over the laundry; and, to his amazement, I never complained as I picked up his dirty socks, put them in the hamper. Once a week, I made clean socks appear, as if by magic, in his dresser drawer.

Our home, our travels, and, our very life together reflected our individual taste; but, we both accepted and enjoyed the fact that our life was filled with willing changes made out of love. We jokingly referred to this as the Bet/Vern factor. Bet/Vern was as real and as important as either of us. Call it what you will, sheer nonsense or a gift from God; either way, I was part of a union of three entities for 42 years. When my husband died, the third entity died with him., and I lost lost both him and Bet/Vern.

The death of any spouse results in a wide range of emotional responses. I've met widow/widowers who readily admit that the death of their spouse was a relief, a welcome freedom, or the best thing that ever happened. At the other end of the spectrum, I've known folks who were in "ho-hum" or really dysfunctional marriages; yet, when their spouse died, they looked me square in the eye and swore that their deceased spouse was wonderful, their marriage was perfect, and they would never get over this great loss. Some of them actually play the poor martyred widow/widower role for the remainder of their life.

The death of a loving, long time, partner brings a unique form of grief. This form of grief sneaks up and catches you unaware. There no predicting what will cause its onset and no way to gauge the intensity of the reaction it produces. About six months after the death of my spouse, I happened to glance at a picture of the two of us and was shocked at the reaction. This picture had sat on my night stand for many years and seeing it was a daily occurrence. On this specific day, I noticed the loving, totally content expression of each of our faces – and BAM! I was remembering the wonderful companionship we shared. Without warning, I realized that this part of my life was gone forever. I couldn't stop crying for hours; I felt like raw hamburger; my heart, soul and mind hurt. The very core of my being felt ripped out. At that moment in time, I would have sold my soul for just 5 minutes snuggled in those sheltering arms.

I hate the need to always be strong; the feeling that nobody has my back; the need to remain alert and stay focused all the time. Damn it- I want to relax a bit - float - just "BE"; I want to drift, unfocus and let go. BUT, don't dare relax; there are things that I have to do to ensure that Vern's expectations of me are met. I must take care of myself, for I am a "widow" - I hate that word, and I hate this

new life that has been thrust upon me. – Journal
entry

Chapter Five

Grieving sucks - it makes you hateful

I'm lost, I'm hurting and I'm striking back at those I love most. To those who still have your mate: I don't like you; you don't appreciate what a wonderful gift it is to be part of a couple. I'm jealous of you, I envy you. You should be happier; can't you see how lucky you are? Be kinder to each other. Be more thoughtful of each others needs and wants. You are just mean and dumb. Damn it! Stop and love each other! Quit trying to change your partner or bitching about their faults or harping at and embarrassing them in public. Why can't you see what you are doing? I hate it that you have each other and I'm all alone. I rant and rave and push people away; then, sanity begins to return and I'm sorry and ashamed. – Journal entry

Never before have I been deliberately hateful and petty. Now, I find my self hurting family members, as well as, belittling grocery checkers, waitresses, and other service providers. I'm rude to anyone who offers me advice or suggestions. In my defense, some people are insensitive and appear to equate being a widow with the inability to think clearly. They ruin their heart felt condolences by adding unsolicited, unwanted, unwelcome, totally silly, and sometimes hurtful advice and suggestions. Of course, this in no way justifies my hateful behavior. I'm shocked by the feelings I'm experiencing; I'm aghast at my behavior; I pray that God will help me rid myself of this hatefulness before I do irreparable harm.

Chapter Six

Grieving sucks – it makes you moody

What is happening to me? I want to give each relative something of Vern's – I almost beg them to take something to remember him by; yet, if they ask about having a specific item, I equate that to being greedy. Where are these mood swings coming from? This is "family". I know they loved him and are hurting too; but, I feel so alone and cast away. I question their feelings for me and often, feel that they think I'm not really a Haines. –Journal entry

At times, I want to forget the past and give away everything that reminds me of the life that my husband and I shared. I want it gone because, remembering my loss hurts too much. I feel that if I get rid of it, I can become numb again and not hurt anymore. At other times, I want to hold on to each little memory and memento of our life together. I experience periods of needing to let go, to allow the past to blur and fade away and get on with whatever my new life is going to be. I also have days when I want to stop the memories from fading. I intentionally recall every little thing about him and our life together. I hold these recollections close and, though this recalling hurts me to the core, I feel the memories are treasures beyond words, and I don't want them to become part of my past. I want my past to come back and bring my spouse with it.

Chapter Seven

Grieving suck – part of "you" is lost

Why can't people understand that when Vern died, the person they knew as "Betty" ceased to exist? I'm no longer that Betty (the one who is part of Bet/Vern) *I'm a lost and confused person. I'm not sure exactly who I am or who I will develop into. When Vern died, so did part of me. They don't get it – they still expect me to think and act like the old me and damn it! I just am not able to do so.* –Journal Entry

I'm becoming increasing aware of subtle changes in the way folks talk and act around me. They are stiff and uptight; their glances and sly questions are sending me mixed messages. More and more, I find myself fighting the urge to just blurt out answers to the questions that I know most of them want answered but are too damned polite to ask.

- Sex? Hell yes, I miss it! I remember that walking on air feeling, the intense excitement of pure uninhibited passion and trust in a partner to give and take pleasure in my body and my emotion. BUT, you don't have to panic or grab your spouse and run! I don't want a casual sex partner. I want to experience the love and trust of deep and mutual desire; once again, I want to feel the joy of being completely open and giving with **_one_** very special person .

- Relax ladies! I don't want your husbands or gentlemen friends. Fact is, I don't even want to be a third (or fifth) wheel at your social gatherings. You can safely invite me for a short visit with no fear that I will spend hours and hours parked on your couch or batting my lashes at your mate. Your husband and your time are safe when I'm around.

• Back off gentlemen! I'm not going to ask you to provide any help with home repair or other "manly" chores. I have family to help with the repairs and when they aren't around, I can afford to hire someone. Thank you for the kind offers; but, I don't need a bed warmer, either.

There are so many times when I ache - physically and spiritually - for someone to kiss my brow, give me a hug, and make the world go away. I just want one short break in this grieving. I want someone to say: "I'm here. I've got you. Nothing will harm you. Let go and let me make it right. Relax, lean on me and let me shelter you for awhile."

When I had a husband, it was OK to tell a friend, "I'm having a bad day, how about a hug"; now, friends look uncomfortable if I admit to having a bad day or ask for a hug. Their hugs have become stiff and brief; it is as if they fear that I may become hysterical and they won't know how to deal with it.

Chapter Eight

Grieving sucks – it makes you afraid

The world is a dumb place and I'm fed up with all the bull shit. These clerks are screwing up customer service and they aren't even smart enough to listen when I try to tell them how to fix the problem. Is the world going crazy or am I? God forgive me, I worry for my sanity. Of course, I don't have all the answers; hell, I can't even take care of myself; yet, I dare lecture others. I'm very afraid that I'm the crazy one. I have to get this under control; it is no good for me or any

***one to function at this level of meanness.
Help me not become a habitually mean
person.*** *Journal entry*

I'm afraid of becoming just another dried up old widow who is forgotten by the world; therefore, I pick fights to get attention. When I have to wait 25 to 30 minutes to get a paper jam in a slot machine fixed, I prance around the casino until I find a service person and when I locate one, I verbally accost him about how I expect better service. I just keep babbling while the poor guy stands there looking totally confused.

At Walmart, my verbal attack is aimed at the checker, and it is so excessive that I actually question my my sanity. I know I need to stop this verbal rampage but I'm helpless to do so. I just keep muttering under my breath about how their service stinks.

When I finally reach a "live" person at my credit union, I become totally belligerent and obnoxious before the person has a chance to speak. When I finally allow the hapless person to speak, I discover that the credit union has "outsourced" their call answering service; and I have just spent 5 minutes intentionally berating someone who is not part of the problem and doesn't even work for my credit union.

There is no excuse for this behavior and I know it. However, there are times when I just don't give a damn and strike out at anyone who tries to do business with me.

I have to get a grip before I do something to disgrace myself and the memory of my spouse.

Chapter Nine

Grieving Sucks - you gotta think money

Some folks (even strangers and casual friends) think they have the right to nose into my financial status. They ask me: "How did Vern leave you set up?" "What's your financial outlook?" "Are you gonna have to sell the house?" "What are you going to do for money?"

How dare they assume that I will tell them these things. It is none of their business. Everybody offers me advice and they all insist

that their way is the only "right way" to handle my money. –Journal entry

Until I became a widow, I never gave finances a second thought. My spouse was an accountant, a whiz at math and a good financial planner. He actually enjoyed managing the budget. I, on the other hand, could add 2+2 and get 5. I considered managing a budget to be a boring and tedious chore that I was happy to avoid. So, he managed the finances and crossed my palm with green stuff often enough to keep me happy (another example of that third entity phenomenon).

While my spouse was alive, I resisted, put off and delayed complying with his request that I at least learn the basics of our finances; consequentially when he passed away, I was totally unprepared to take on this responsibility.

As soon as I became a widow, I asked my brother-in-law to give me a crash course in finance. Thank God that he understands the world of finance, understands his brother's filing system and was willing to teach me the basics of these things.

At the worst possible time, I had to struggle to comprehend some major facts of life, I needed to know if I had enough to live on, if I needed to go back into the workforce and/or what, if any, other life altering changes I was going to need to make right away. All I wanted to do was crawl in a hole, pull the cover over it and stay there; yet, I had no choice but to hit the deck running and deal with things like:

- Paying routine bills and expenses (even using on-line banking)

- Understanding my monthly cash flow (actually learning what cash flow was)

- Covering unexpected bills (sure was not expecting to cover a life-flight helicopter bill so soon. A *sad, but true fact:* Even when the patient dies prior to being placed in the helicopter, if one is requested, you have to pay)

- Learning the language of the financial world. All those new terms and acronyms (TOD/Transfer on

Death – CD – MRD/Minimum Required Distribution
- Mutual Fund – IRA – Estate Tax - Prime Rate – Tax
Rate – Mortgage Rate- etc.)

- Dealing with insurance, death benefits, wills,
  attorneys, County/State officials, etc.

- **Wondering why every damned body I do business
  with needs a Death Certificate - "original copy
  with a state seal on it"!!** Do these folks really think
  anyone in their right mind would lie about the death of
  a spouse? (A word to the wise, regarding Death
  Certificates: You better order lots of these – you are
  going to need them).

*I'm sure that I've gained a few relatives
who think they should have a piece of the pie.
I wonder, if I were broke how many would
want to share their pie with me? - Journal entry*

*I have no memory of writing the above entry in my journal;
however, when I read it, I realized how genuine the feeling is and*

decided to include it in this book in hope that some folks will see just how hurtful hints for handouts can be to a new widow/widower.

Chapter Ten

Grieving sucks - self confidence goes

Feeling restless. I have to be doing something, but I'm not sure what to do. Wheels in my mind won't stop spinning; yet, there is no traction. I'm drifting, lost and filled with a sense of impending doom. -Journal entry

The advice that I first and most consistently received following the death of my spouse was: "Don't make any major decisions for at least a year". Unfortunately, this is the dumbest thing anyone can suggest. Fortunately, one of the first lessons I learned from grief is that this specific bit of advice is impossible to follow. First, I discovered that making any decision while my mind was still reeling from the loss of my spouse was a major decision. Second, I found that life continued whether I wanted it to or not. Yes, life goes on and, because decisions are part of life, they must be dealt with.

You have to decide how many death certificates to order; you have to decide which bills to pay right away and which can wait 'til later; you have to feed, house and reassure visiting family members. Then, you must deal with official notifications and forms (lots of forms); ***another note to readers:*** the information that you put on these forms, as well as the way in which you word the information, influences your cash flow and your taxes. The bottom line is some decisions can't be put off without serious consequences.

The advice I wish that I had received is: "You're going to have to weigh options and make decisions, and you won't always select the wisest option; so, put off the decisions that you can; make the ones that you must, and don't worry about the mistakes. You will make mistakes; but, mistakes are correctable."

By attempting to avoid making decisions (or allowing others to make them for me), and coupling that with my fear of making mistakes I caused myself so much frustration, worry and panic that I became physically ill. If someone had reminded me that making mistakes was inevitable and, had I received assurance that I could correct or overcome those mistakes, things would have been so much easier and less painful for me.

SECTION II

OR DOES IT?

Introduction

In the days immediately following the sudden death of my husband, I searched the net for a book, an article, a sermon, or anything that might help to soothe my aching heart and help me to begin the impossible task of going on without him. I was surprised at just how many experts (I use the term loosely) I found out there in cyberspace.

I found an abundance of data on grief and grieving; I found clinical descriptions of everything from *"Anticipatory grief"*(dealing with the pain one feels when considering moving, divorce, putting a pet to sleep, etc.) to *"Acute grief"* (dealing with impossible loss). I even found advice on dealing with *"Chronic grief"* (whatever the hell that is).

Upon closer examination, I discovered that most of the information, in the books and on the internet, was superficial, poorly thought out, and meaningless. I'm sure the individuals who took the time to share this information were well meaning; but, much of it was misplaced, trivial, or just plain false. Very quickly, I learned to shun the internet gurus and ignore most of the advice of well meaning friends and relatives. Through trial and error, I discovered what worked best for me. Not surprisingly, most of what worked best for me had been learned at my Grandma Freeman's knee. I had a talk with my pal God. I asked Him to guide me and I trusted in Him to do so. I soon came to the realization that I had to grieve one step at a time and not let the big picture overwhelm me.

Taking grief one step at a time eased my panic, slowed my racing mind, and helped me accept that many valuable lessons can only be learned after experiencing great pain.

Sharing so much of my life with my husband has greatly enriched it; and, given the choice, I would opt to keep him by my side and forgo the lessons to be learned from profound grief. Of course, that isn't an option.

Working my way through grief has rendered me a different person, indeed, a stronger, more productive, and happier person. I'm grateful for the lessons that grieving taught me. These lessons will serve me well for the remainder of my life and will help make life easier and more exciting for me.

I have arrived at the point where I'm able to re-examine my earlier statement that GRIEVING SUCKS and ask myself:

OR DOES IT?

Chapter Eleven

Grieving teaches you to give up

Happy New Year? Yeah, right! OK, God, I really surrender – I give up. I'm in a hole and I have no will to come out – in fact, it is comfortable down here. As the old country song says, "I'm on the back side of 30 (well, 70)*, the short side of time. I'm back on the bottom with no will to climb." Vern is gone.* **Cecil** (the father of my children) *is gone. JP (my youngest son) is dying and his siblings pick his father's death bed to stage an "intervention".* **Rick** (my first born) *has just been diagnosed*

with diabetes. My friends are few and far between. I've lost interest in Writer's Gallery (my local news paper column). **I don't want to die; however, I don't want to put forth the effort to really live. Seems every time I think that I've really slain this damned dragon, the darned thing grows another head and comes at me again. I'm not really sad, or mad, or even frustrated; I simply don't care anymore. I'm back to square one. I'm numb; and, I don't know what to do about it; nor do I have the desire or energy to keep trying to learn. Please, life, just go away and let me sit here! Damn it! I just can't take much more of this being brave crap – I need someone to take care of me and help me with this. It is just too much for me to handle.** _Journal entry_

Ushering in a new year as a widow was traumatic for me. I could no longer deny the passage of time. Life was continuing and it was propelling me further away from the safe little niche that I enjoyed as a beloved wife.

Chapter Twelve

Grieving teaches you to take inventory

After I gave up and decided to stop trying, the hole into which I had crawled began to feel uncomfortable; so, I forced myself to stop my pity party long enough to take inventory of my feelings. This is great therapy and I recommend that everyone (not just widow/widowers) do this periodically. The act of taking inventory clarified a number of things for me:

A) I'm still fumbling around, like a silly child, wanting to wish all the fear and confusion away. Yet, I'm beginning to realize that I have to deal with my emotions and start making the hard decisions. The easy, no brainier ones have already taken care of themselves, some by default. I have accepted the fact that my spouse isn't coming back to make any of the decisions for me and I've given up on the dream that there is a knight in shining armor just waiting to take on the job of making Betty happy. It is now time to take hold and direct my own fate.

B) I'm lonesome in ways that I never have been before. I miss the companionable, shared silences; I miss the time we spent watching a TV program or a sunset, listening to the peaceful sound of water moving over rocks in a creek bed or the roar of a waterfall. I miss the routines that were so "us" (Wednesday = grocery shopping, weekdays at 5 pm = watch O'Reiley, Thursday = buffet lunch and slots). I miss our long (or short) drives and just being together.

C) My relationship with in-laws is still troublesome. My mood swings are extreme. For many years I enjoyed the security of knowing that I was part of my husband's family; now, I'm not sure those feelings were mutual; I suspect that some of his family members don't like me at all. I hate feeling so alone and unsure of how I currently fit into this family. I hate the feeling of being cast off by certain in-laws. At times I question whether some some of them really loved my spouse. He was their blood; if they didn't really love him, I can only imagine how the feel about me.

D) Losing a spouse is so final. I got no chance to beg for him to stay alive, no chance to hold and nurse him. It was just done and over before I could even comprehend what was happening. I am alone; alone is so hard. Alone means I'm part of nothing; I have no partner, no special pal, no soul-mate; I'm just alone.

E) I always feel there is something that I have left undone, something that my spouse expected me to do. I feel desperate to identify what I need to do to meet those expectations. Plus, I'm afraid that if I give in and relax, I'm lost forever in a sea of nothingness.

F) The emerging me is very vulnerable. I'm facing the world alone; I'm like a new born kitten shaky, weak, scared, excited, exposed, open. I'm like a blank page waiting to be written on. I want to prove I can handle being alone, that I can take care of myself, that I can travel alone and that I can hone my focus and stay on track. Some days, I think that in doing OK and I'll soon begin to feel happy and upbeat again. Other days, I feel guilty about anticipating happiness. I'm not sure that I'm ready for this new life; BUT, I'm pretty sure this new life is happening whether I'm ready or not. I just have to hang on and see where it all leads.

Chapter Thirteen

Grieving teaches you "baby steps"

Dear God, I don't know who I am? I'm so used to getting Vern's input about what <u>we</u> will do, how <u>we</u> dress, what do <u>we</u> eat (want a snack or a full meal?), where do <u>we</u> eat (cook at home, go out, order in?). Now I wonder how much of me is solely me , the way I really want to be, and how much is influenced by <u>we</u> thinking? -Journal entry

When I realized that my thinking pattern was still very much that of a wife, I was rocked to the core. If left unchecked, this thinking pattern will hinder my ability to reclaim my independent thought process. I must force myself to ask/examine the question: "What am I going to be, now that I'm not a wife?" Do I hold on to what "used to be", keep thinking like a wife, and live in the past; or, do I adjust my thinking to match my current situation?

The discovery that I had no ready answer to these questions, highlighted the fact that I wasn't as self assured as I perceived myself to be. This discovery prompted me to get on with the adjustment process. The journal entry below, indicates the beginning of my "baby steps" toward more independent thinking.

Why do I keep getting tight curly perms and having my hair cut so short? Duh! You dummy, that is the way Vern likes your hair; not the way you like it. He isn't here to look at it any longer – so change it. – Journal entry

Changing my hair style was an easy decision; nonetheless, it confirmed that I was in the process of becoming a different person; I couldn't avoid it; so, I may as well embrace it and recognize that I could define just who this new person would be. Knowing this gave me a jolt of optimism.

Chapter Fourteen

Grieving teaches humility

What a snob I have been. Judging elderly women so harshly, looking down my nose at the ones who spent time playing bingo, sneeringly referring to them as the "bingo bunch", seeing them as silly, frivolous, little old ladies, and pitying them for having such a dull and boring life. My misplaced pity and snobbery even extended to little old ladies pushing wheeled carts home from their solitary shopping trips. –Journal entry

It is interesting how grief can humble a person. Now that I have no loving partner, I'm much less judgmental. I'm not a spring chicken; but, there is life in this old girl. Part of me longs to become part of a spirited, fun loving group. Now, when I gaze into the bingo hall, I no longer consider those little old ladies to be silly and frivolous. They appear to be involved in life; they are sharing companionship, laughter and good will. That has to beat sitting home with only the TV for company.

As for the little old ladies with the wheeled carts, I've joined them. Walking is good exercise; and I enjoy strolling to my neighborhood Walmart. Furthermore, after experiencing a few sore shoulders from carrying my purchases home; I see the wisdom of those little wheeled carts.

Chapter Fifteen

Grieving reduces fear of the unknown

The worst has happened. Vern is dead and I'm alone with nobody to lean on; wonder of wonders, I'm surviving it. WOW! This old bird is tougher than I suspected. - Journal entry

The realization that I had withstood what I previously assumed would be a mortal blow, the death of my spouse, freed a log jam of emotions inside me. I no longer waste so much of my time anticipating future disasters. I concentrate on preparing myself to handle current problems. The panic that I felt, immediately following my spouses death, is beginning to fade. Each day I become a little less fearful of the unknown.   More and more often, I'm discovering a new found confidence in myself and a feeling of hopefulness that I can and will develop the ability to survive and thrive on my own.

Chapter Sixteen

Grieving teaches you to get up

Today is Vern's birthday and I'm sad, alone, and afraid. I thought I had things under control; but, I'm overwhelmed by taxes. I'm completely unprepared to deal with this issue and fear that I'll screw it up and land in jail. I've mastered paying the bills, managing my budget, sleeping alone in that big, lonely bed, and socializing without partner; now, I'm faced with dealing with the IRS. Yes, trying to *figure out my taxes scares the hell out of me. I've seen what can happen if/when the IRS decides you are trying to cheat them. I feel trapped, incompetent, stupid, and abandoned. I need someone to come rescue me. I've bottomed out and I can't do this by myself. - Journal entry*

This was another break through day for me, a day of more baby steps. I forced myself to pause and remember that each person is ultimately responsible for the choices they make. That was a powerful and scary thought; The absolute, unavoidable fact is, I'm the only one who can choose whether to wallow in doubt and self-pity or not. God granted me the free will to make choices. He gave me the brains to figure out that the quality of my life is directly tied to the choices that I make! Today, this minute, I get to choose what actions I will take:

- Am I going to sit at my desk playing computer games to distract myself and avoid facing my problems?

- Am I going to spend my time crying, feeling sorry for myself, and complaining that life isn't fair?

- Am I going to moan about the knot of fear and tension that produces pain in the middle of my belly?

- Am I going to waste another day being afraid to make choices?

- What if I make the wrong choice? (So, I make another one.)

- What if I make the current situation worse? (So what! Come on, life ain't so great right now.)

- Isn't it time to wake up and accept that I'm responsible for nobody but myself? (Better yet, shouldn't I consider that nobody but me is responsible for me?)

This series of questions led me to the conclusion that only I have the ability to stop filling my mind with resentment, disappointment, fear, etc. Each choice I make and each action I take (or don't take) has consequences; because God gives me free will to make choices and take actions, I alone am responsible for the consequences of these choices and actions. Today I choose to accept responsibility for my choices. I know that with my pal God on my side, I'll be OK.

Today, I take care of the tax situation. I ain't superman and I don't know how to do taxes; I do know a bit about hiring folks and I'm gonna hire the best CPA I can find to do my taxes.

Eureka! I've found it! The smart choice is: Give up – give in - give it to God! Now, GET UP and learn to "Do your best and let Him do the rest". *–Journal entry*

Chapter Seventeen

Grieving helps reset default thinking

Default thinking occurs when your mind goes into neutral and you are not purposely focusing your thoughts. The following journal entries are examples of just how volatile my default thinking was at one point in my grieving:

- _September 22:_ **I think I have a grip. I really think I get it!!! Slept like a rock last evening. Thank God! Yes, from the bottom of my heart, I Thank you Lord. I'm going to work at ridding myself of the notion that the world is out to get** *me and begin shaping up my attitude. Vern's dead; I'm alive; I get it! The world isn't trying to make me feel stupid, or bad; nor, is it treating me wrong. Nothing and nobody is "out to get me". My thoughts, beliefs, and faith are going to make or break my mental health. I'm the one who can stop this paranoia. I have to devote my efforts to moving back to a more healthy and happier frame of mind. With God's help I'll make it through this crazy phase.* - *Journal entry*

- <u>September 26:</u> **For the past week**: *I've felt that I was near the end of the road with this grieving thing; yet, just when I'm starting to feel strong, almost invincible, I discover that I'm* *wrong. Now, I've hit a curve in the road! Bits of my day-to-day life are changing and I'm spending less time thinking of the way things used to be. BUT, I'm not   ready to have the feeling of being a wife go away. I know I can't go back there (oh what joy if only I could). Perhaps, I'll just concentrate on what used to be, not on the future. Maybe, I don't want to go on from here. BUT, I don't think I should live in the past. Maybe I should give in to the urge to "get a life"* (as the kids keep saying) *and try to get me a happy exciting one. BUT, I don't know what I want that life to be like or how I can make it happen and that scares the hell out of me* -Journal entry

- <u>September 29:</u> *I'm so tired of this emotional roller coaster. One minute up, next minute down; want to relax, afraid to relax. I'm worried that if I relax and allow my mind to wander, I may go "round the bin" and be unable to refocus on the real world. This kind of behavior has to stop – today, I will begin resetting my default thinking.*
-Journal entry

Resetting default thinking is not as difficult as some people pretend; nor, is the process or doing so the same for everyone. Anyone desiring to reset their default thinking, can get help doing so; just do a quick Google, using the key phrase "positive thinking" or "default thinking".

During my grieving, I've developed very negative thinking patterns, and my doctor has told me that this is beginning to take a toll on my physical health. I've learned another lesson from grief: negative thinking injures your health.

To reset my default thinking and improve my physical health, I must gain control of my emotions. To do this, I've opted to use self-talk. By this I mean, I will force myself to sit quietly and let my mind drift (after so many months of forcing myself to to stay focused, this is a frightening, but I must do it). As my thoughts drift, they inevitability become muddled, frantic and negative; this is where self-talk begins. I mentally say to myself: *"Halt! Stop that thought pattern! Contentment is a better thought; concentrate on becoming content. Suspicion, fear, lack of faith are learned behaviors –* **unlearn them.** *Default to contentment. You were a happy contented child and teen – learn to think like that again."*

Chapter Eighteen

Grieving helps you face reality

God, I'm sure that I will thank you later for sending Rick to live with me. Right now, I just don't care. In my heart, I'm grateful that I don't have to be totally alone in this big silent house; but, I'm not able to communicate that to Rick, yet. Right now, I'm acting like an ungrateful old witch who can't get it together. I don't want to live with anyone except Vern. I don't want to change my life or my daily routine. I don't want to be a widow. I don't like my new life. I want my old one back. -Journal entry

It was nothing short of a miracle that my son was willing to completely revamp his life, move to the desert and live with me; additionally, it was amazing that he did so immediately following my husband's death. In spite of this miracle, I couldn't stop feeling sorry for myself long enough to be grateful I was like a child having a tantrum: "I want what I want, when I want it, and nothing else will do!"

Fortunately, I have couple of very special friends who allowed me rant, rave, and work my way past the tantrum stage. Thanks to their help, I began to face the reality of being a widow and the need to build a new life.

My old buddy BJ is my hero; and, just like in old RCMP movies, she keeps coming to my rescue, except she doesn't ride a white steed

when she does it. She just points me in the right direction and keeps pushing 'til I move that way. - Journal entry

While I don't expect that I will ever like being a widow; I'm able to face the reality of it and, as I predicted in my journal, I'm able to honestly thank God that my son is with me. I'm slowly adapting to a new life style and building a room-mate relationship with my son. This works for both of us and compliments the mother/son relationship that we have always enjoyed.

Chapter Nineteen

Grieving helps you focus on the present

"It is difficult to live in the present, ridiculous to live in the future, and impossible to live in the past. Nothing is as far away as one minute ago. (Jim Bishop)

Until I read the quote above, I had never heard of Jim Bishop. I still don't know who he was/is or why the author quoted him. Nonetheless, his words speak volumes to me. Many times in my life, I've been advised to "live in the moment". I understand the concept and see the wisdom that advice; but, it begs the question: "How, exactly, do I do that?"

Until recently, I had a tendency to spend more time thinking of the future than enjoying the present moment. I considered it wise to spend time worrying about what could possibly happen in the future and preparing myself to cope with it. Over the years, this habit robbed me of many enjoyable moments that I could have experienced while I was a wife.

Grieving has taught me to stay a bit longer in the present moment. I've reduced the amount of time I spend creating fearful scenarios or imagining future crisis. Instead, I remind myself that worrying about the future or regretting the past isn't going to change what has been or what will be. I focus on the positive things that are happening in my life – _at this moment._ I allow myself time to fully absorb the moment before I move on to the next moment. When I do move to the next moment, I do so with a fundamental trust that it is going to be alright, even when I haven't planned for it.

Chapter Twenty

Grieving reinforces lifelong learning

A very important lesson that I have learned from experiencing such profound grief is that learning doesn't cease because of age. Learning ceases because we become lazy, set in our ways, or too comfortable in our rut. We stop learning when we lose confidence in our ability to master new things. In my case, I ceased learning because I was so comfortable and satisfied with the life that my husband and I shared that I had little motivation or time for new people, experiences. or activities. Together we read, traveled; did a little gourmet cooking, listened to music, gardened, played the penny slots, watched sunrise/sunsets, and had wonderful conversations with each other. Friends said we were "joined at the hip". They were right, and we liked it that way.

When I became a widow, I was left with two options; 1) continue to exclude new people and new experiences from my life, or, 2) expand my horizons and become open to new people, experiences, and activities. I opted to expand my horizons and what a learning experience this expansion is offering me. I'm making new friends and reconnecting with old ones; I'm trying new activities and reviving interest in old ones; I'm learning to respect my physical limitations, but daring to test those limits.

Chapter Twenty One

Grieving brings surprises

Kelly, invited me to attend a financial presentation sponsored by Lord Abbett & Company. Surprise! I really enjoyed the presentation; I understood most of the theories presented and learned a bunch of new words and phrases that make it a little easier to understand my finances. -Journal entry

I was shocked at how comfortable I felt in this group of "finance people". I was surprised at how easily I picked up the language and how much I enjoyed participating in the discussion that followed the presentation. I'm no longer frightened and intimidated when conversations turn to finances, stocks, bonds, annuities, investments, etc. I've surprised myself by gaining a real desire to better understand my personal finances. After years of professing to be bored by the subject, I find I want to learn more about the world of finance and how I can take a pro-active role in managing my investments.

Chapter Twenty Two

Grieving teaches it is OK to have fun

Today, I laughed out loud. Yep, I had an old fashioned giggle fit for the first time since becoming a widow . It felt right! It felt good! It felt natural! -Journal entry

I learned a long time ago that attempting to share the cause of a giggle fit usually results in one of those awkward "guess, you had to be there " moments; so, I won't attempt to share the reason for my laughter. Let's just leave it at this, laughter happened because I finally learned the ***most important*** *lesson* that grieving teaches: **IT IS OK TO HAVE FUN AGAIN!**

Experiencing spontaneous laughter seemed to mark the end of my acute grief. It reinforced that there can be meaningful life after the loss of a spouse.

Grieving has helped me rediscover the importance of fun and play in my life. I'm becoming less afraid to engage in activities just for fun.   I'm learning to do things that are completely spontaneous, carefree, and silly without feeling self-conscious or looking around to see if others are judging me for my "childish" behavior.

Living life to the fullest is more important to me than worrying about the judgment of others. I've been a *responsible adult* for a very long time. Even now, I have no intention of becoming irresponsible or failing to remain contributing member of society.   Nonetheless, I intend increase the number of occasions upon which I let me hair down, kick up my heels, and play. I consider the ability to play and find joy in playing a blessing from God. It uplifts the soul, and elevates the quality of life. So, from this day forward, I'm giving myself the gift of play.

I recognize that play is not without risks; it requires that you open your heart and mind to your playmate(s); it requires that you give up false pride and fault finding; it involves childlike trust and openness. I'm willing to take those risks.

As of today, I'm proclaiming it unnecessary, unwise and unhealthy to condemn playfulness as "being childish", I'm declaring that life is much easier and more enjoyable when I allow myself time for unstructured play sessions. I intend to play a little every day. I'll let my imagination run wild and free, and see the world once again with a sense of wonder and awe.

Epilog

Grieving teaches you to get on with it

I expect that I'll always feel occasional pangs of grief over the loss of Vern. But, memories of our shared good times soften the feelings of sadness caused by his loss and I'm content with the lessons learned from my grieving. -Journal entry

Of all the emotions that I've experienced in my lifetime, I find grief to be the most complex and least understood. For me grieving has produced everything from mild episodes of "the blues", to heart pounding, gut wrenching pain that felt as though it were ripping me to shreds. Plus, I've experienced entire spectrum of emotions in between those two extremes.

The grief caused by the loss of a loving spouse or a child is, without a doubt, among the most painful emotion that exists. Nonetheless, I disagree with those who say that it is the ultimate sorrow. As painful as this type grief is, I believe that the ultimate sorrow is failing to learn from it. Failure to learn how to pick up the pieces and get on with life is the ultimate sorrow; plus, it is disrespectful to the deceased.

In a perfect world, there would be no grief. Unfortunately, the world we inhabit is not perfect and it is more likely than not that each of us will experience profound grief during our lifetime.

Does GRIEVING SUCK?

YES!!

Are there valuable lessons to be learned from this grieving?

ABSOLUTELY, YES!